A NOTE FROM THE PUBLISHER

Scots is a language with a long history and a rich
literature. It is a highly descriptive language with
regional variations in vocabulary, pronunciation
and spelling. Many words are onomatopoeic and
fizz with meaning, but some simply cannot be
translated into English. However, the illustrations
in this wee book capture the spirit of the
language. Enjoy.

D0767114

Dae ye ken?

VICKI GAUSDEN

Luath Press Ltd
EDINBURGH

www.luath.co.uk

First published 2006

ISBN (10): 1-905222-59-9
ISBN (13): 978-1-9-0522259-9

The paper used in this book is produced from
renewable forests and is chlorine-free.

Printed and bound by
Bell & Bain Ltd., Glasgow

For my parents who mostly didn't panic when I told them I was going to art college.

With thanks to Chris Robinson, Director of Scottish Language Dictionaries, and her team. They have a website at www.scotsdictionaries.org.uk. The Scottish National Dictionary and A Dictionary of the Older Scottish Tongue can be consulted free online at www.dsl.ac.uk.

Contents

Fowk

people

Bausy

large,
corpulent

Gallus

cheeky

Canny

Cautious

Clip-cloot

a gossip

Drouthy

thirsty

Greet

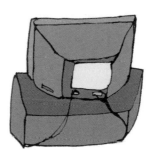

weep

Haivers

THE END IS NIGH

talks
nonsense

Peelie -wallie

delicate, sickly

Wabbit

tired

Gang oot on the toon

Go for a night out

Howff

meeting place

Doch n doris

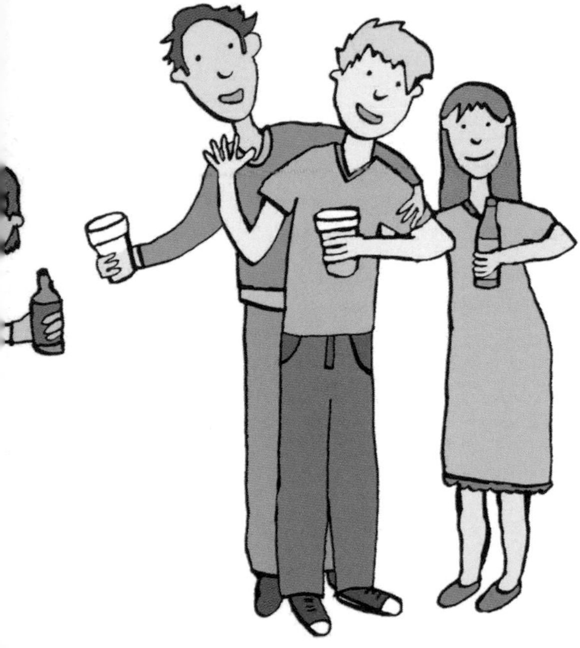

farewell drink

Birl

brisk dance

Lawin

bill,
reckoning

Brulzie

brawl,
commotion

Polis

POLICE STOP

police

The wee sma oors

the early hours

Raivelled

muddled, untidy

Gaun the messages

going shopping

Aits

oats

Baurley
-bree

whisky

Clootie dumpling

steamed pudding

Ingan

Onion

Gigot

leg

of mutton

Mealie pudden

oatmeal pudding

Piece

sandwich

Tatties

POTATO

potatoes

Kith and kin

relations and family

Auld
-faither

grandfather

Auld-mither

grandmother

Bidie-in

live-in partner

Callant

lad

Ghaist

ghost

Sherrack

noisy quarrel

Wean

child

Wi bairn

pregnant

Muckle beasts & wee beasties

large animals & small animals

Baudrons

cat

Corbie

Crow

Emmertins

ants

Ettercap

spider

Mowdiewort

mole

Pownie

pony

Sea-maw

Seagull

Tod

fox

Ahint

behind

Bide

stay

Gloamin

dusk,
twilight

Keek-o
-day

dawn

Kirk

Church

Tae

towards

Vaige

journey

Widdershins

anti-clockwise

Pairts o the bodie

parts of the body

Bahookie

posterior

Een

eyes

Elbuck

elbow

Fuit

foot

Harns

brains

Heid

head

Mowser

moustache

oxter

armpit

Wallies

false teeth

Wame

stomach

Words fir the wather

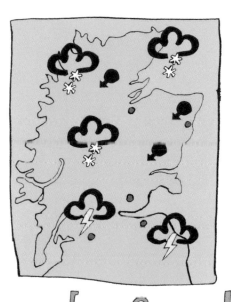

words for the weather

Cranreuch

white frost

Dreich

dull

Glousterie

gusty, blustering

Smirr

drizzle

Thunner - plump

Sudden downpour

Yowdendrift

wind driven snow

About Me

I doodled all over my notebooks as a child at school and soon realised that true happiness could be found with a pen in one hand and a blank sheet of paper in the other. I studied for a BA (Hons) Illustration at Edinburgh College of Art and graduated in 2005. I am now living in Edinburgh and working as a Freelance Illustrator and Hand-Lettering Artist. I work mainly from my own head, imagining scenarios and trying to make myself laugh. I love meeting new people and explaining to them what I do for a living.

www.vickigausden.co.uk